The Return *of* Christendom

Demography, Politics, and the Coming Christian Majority

STEPHEN R. TURLEY, PH.D.

TURLEY TALKS

A New Conservative Age is Rising
www.TurleyTalks.com

Table of Contents

The Return of Christendom

Everywhere one looks today in the West, it appears that proponents of secular liberalism are celebrating another social victory lap. So-called same-sex marriage, over 50 self-identifying gender options on Facebook, lawsuits against Christian bakers and florists, 'gender neutral' public restroom laws, abortion on demand, collectively constitute a daily reminder that our world is changing in ways unimaginable just a few decades back. For those of us who believe that our historic customs, cultures, and religious traditions represent faithful visions of the true, the good, and the beautiful in ways indispensable to the cultivation of wisdom and virtue, this brave new world appears increasingly alien. Many of us feel like strangers in our own countries. At work, we can't open our mouths without the fear of potentially being fired from our jobs because our comments were deemed offensive, bigoted, or homophobic.

It's no wonder that many conservatives in the West are rather hopelessly pessimistic about the future of civilization. In his farewell speech to the Focus on the Family staff, James Dobson defeatedly admitted: "We tried to defend the unborn child, the dignity of the family, but it was a holding action. ... We are awash in evil, and the battle is still to be waged. We are right now in the most discouraging period of that long conflict. Humanly speaking, we can say we have lost all those battles."[1] Douglas Murray warns that "Europe is in the process of committing suicide ... by the end of the lifespans of most people currently alive, Europe will not be Europe, and the peoples of Europe will have lost the only place in the world we had to call home."[2] And Rod Dreher laments: "The light of Christianity is flickering out all over the West. There are people alive today who may live to see the effective death of Christianity within our civilization."[3]

While fully acknowledging the disappointments and challenges that have engendered such dire prognostications,[4] I want to argue that there is a radically different way of looking at our current context. I believe these rather distressing predictions are contradicted by an astonishing backlash currently underway throughout the West that does not indicate a defeat but a renewal; not a death but a rebirth. I want to argue that we are actually seeing nothing less than a conservative Christian resurgence in our demographics and politics that promises not suicide but rather the salvation of the West.

The Return of Religion

A growing number of journalists and scholars are observing that religious nationalism is making a comeback. A quick internet search reveals articles such as "How Religion Made a Global Comeback in 2017," "The Rise of Religious Nationalism in India," "Christian Nationalism in Your Statehouse," and so on. A recent article published in *The Atlantic* focused broadly on the global comeback of

---

[1] https://washingtonmonthly.com/2009/04/12/dobson-points-to-culture-war-defeat/.
[2] Douglas Murry, The Strange Death of Europe: Immigration, Identity, Islam (London: Bloomsbury, 2017), 1.
[3] Rod Dreher, The Benedict Option: A Strategy for Christians in a Post-Christian Nation (New York: Random House, 2017).
[4] For an extended treatment of our current political and cultural context, see my *The Triumph of Tradition: How the Resurgence of Religion is Reawakening a Conservative World* (Newark: Turley Talks Publishing, 2018).

religion throughout the world, but particularly in the administration of President Trump.[5] The author notes that the religious focus of Trump's administration was on full display in his first international trip as president, where he visited Jerusalem, Riyadh, and Rome framed explicitly as a world tour of the Abrahamic religions.

The Trump administration is hardly unique in this respect. In Central Europe, Poland's Catholic bishops recently held a formal ceremony before their president declaring Jesus Christ as King and Lord over their nation; and the Hungarian Prime Minister, Viktor Orban, has proclaimed Hungary a 'Christian Democracy' dedicated to defending Christian civilization over and against the secular globalization represented by the European Union. Eastern European nations such as Georgia have reintroduced Orthodox Christianity back into their public-school curriculum, and Igor Dodon, president of Moldova, has recommitted his nation to the supremacy of Christian values. In post-Soviet Russia, the Russian Orthodox Church has risen to a political prominence not seen since the days of the tsars. And even in the Pacific, officials in Samoa have declared their island a Christian nation by revising their constitution as dedicated explicitly to the Holy Trinity.

A Re-Christianized Europe?

These recent developments may seem rather surprising given that scholars have thus far focused more on the geographic relocation of Christianity *away* from Europe and more towards the global south.[6] While these developments are certainly impressive, other scholars, such as sociologist Rodney Stark and

[5] Emma Green, "Trump Begins His Religion World Tour," https://www.theatlantic.com/international/archive/2017/05/trump-israel-saudi-arabia-vatican/527310/.
[6] See, for example, Philip Jenkins, The Next Christendom: The Coming of Global Christianity (Oxford: Oxford University Press, 2011).

demographer Eric Kaufmann, have noticed that the geographic center of Christianity may not be relocating quite the way others anticipated.[7] There is, in fact, a very significant undercurrent of growing Christian sentiment in the geographic West that appears to be driven by at least two dominant dynamics. First, there is an extraordinary demographic revolution taking place that is significantly changing the religious complexion of the West in favor of conservative Christian values, and secondly, there is growing political discontent with the secularized globalist world order, accompanied by a marked return to traditional values and ways of life. We can see these two developments as the consequences of the inherent futilities or contradictions within secularized globalization, twin futilities that will be helpful to briefly explore.

Globalization and Its Demographic Resistance

The conception of globalism or globalization is widely recognized as a vast interlocking mechanism of technology and telecomm-unications that creates a single worldwide economic and political system.[8] As such, globalization reorganizes the world according to a number of specific characteristics that are uniquely transnational and translocal. Think, for example, of your local mall; in one sense, the mass shopping complex is, in fact, local in terms of its proximity to consumers, but notice that the retail outlets that comprise the various stores at a mall are *not* local but rather national and international chains and brand names. This is especially the case with the latest releases at the movie theater or the offerings at the food court. This is disembedding: from the

---

[7] Rodney Stark, The Triumph of Faith: Why the World is More Religious than Ever (Wilmington, DE: ISI Books, 2015); Eric Kaufmann, Shall the Religious Inherit the Earth? Demography and Politics in the Twenty-First Century (London: Profile Books, 2010).

[8] Anthony Giddens, Runaway World: How Globalization is Reshaping our Lives (New York: Routledge, 2000).

ubiquity of 'Made in China' imprints on our products and consumables, to the mass influx of immigrant labor, both legal and illegal, and the ever-increasing 'Orlando-ization' of our urban and suburban landscapes by chains and franchises; our lives are increasingly defined and interpreted by translocal economic and social processes.

However, it is not merely economic processes that have been arrested from provincial control; such dislodging also involves localized customs, traditions, languages, and religions. Whereas pre-modern societies are characterized generally by provincial beliefs and practices considered sacred and absolute, globalized societies offer a range of consumer-based options that call into question the sanctity of local beliefs and practices, relativizing them to a 'global food court' of many other creedal alternatives.

This social order of consumer-based options tends to forge a new conception of the human person as a sovereign individual who exercises control over his or her own life circumstances.[9] Traditional social structures and arrangements are generally fixed in terms of key identity markers such as gender, sexual orientation, and religious affiliation. But globalized societies, because of the wide array of options, see this fixedness as restrictive. And so traditional morals and customs tend to give way to what we called *lifestyle values*. Lifestyle values operate according to a plurality of what sociologist Peter Berger defines as 'life-worlds,' wherein each individual practices whatever belief system deemed most plausible by him or her. These belief systems include everything from religious identity to gender identity and, of course, marriage.

---

[9] Anthony Giddens, *Modernity and Self-Identity: Self and Society in the Late Modern Age* (Stanford, CA: Stanford University Press, 1991), 211.

So, it goes without saying that the advent of lifestyle values has radically redefined the whole notion of marriage. Over the last several decades, marriage has been reinterpreted solely as a legal contract that satisfies the needs of intimacy between the attracted persons. Marriage simply no longer has any objective or traditional definition but is rather defined by those in a relationship with one another according to their personal beliefs and values. And what we've found is that personal beliefs and values *have the right not to procreate.* As a result, fertility rates have dropped dramatically in the West, and in nations such as Spain and Portugal, whole populations have actually begun to shrink. Indeed, birthrates have declined so rapidly and so widely across the European continent that pundits are openly recognizing that without a major baby boom, Europe is headed for a population disaster.[10]

And yet, a major baby boom is precisely what we are seeing, but not across the board, as it were; fertility is flourishing, particularly among *conservative Christian* women. As we'll discover below, conservative Christians are having upwards of four children for every one child born to secular non-religious couples. In France, for example, 30 percent of French women, predominantly conservative Catholic, are responsible for over 50 percent of all births in France. Such a fertility discrepancy not only promises to avert the population disaster widely prognosticated for the continent *but is already radically altering its demographic makeup in favor of conservative Christian sentiments and values.*

---

[10] See, for example, Ashifa Kassam, et al, "Europe needs many more babies to avert a population disaster," https://www.theguardian.com/world/2015/aug/23/baby-crisis-europe-brink-depopulation-disaster.

Globalization and Its Political Resistance

The second futility of globalization revolves around the distinctively *secular* dynamics intrinsic to globalization; such dynamics turn out to be inconsistent with a sustainable social order, thus driving an increasing number of nations back to their religious foundations.

Since the work of sociologist Emile Durkheim, scholars have widely recognized that all social order is rooted in what Durkheim called the *sacred*: socially ubiquitous rules, understandings, and goals considered by a population to be absolute and unquestionable.[11] The inviolability of such rules, understandings, and goals provides the very order by which society is constituted. What this means is that there is an inescapable religious character to be found in every aspect of social life, such as notions of private property, money, national rituals, education, science, and the like, a religious character that pre-industrialized society took rather for granted.[12]

With the advent of globalization, there arose a social dynamic inherent in globalized processes called *detraditionalization,* or various mechanisms by which local customs and traditions are relativized to wider economic, scientific, and technocratic forces.[13] Once social life is caught up in a global industrialized economic system, it is propelled away from traditional, national, and local practices and beliefs, rendering its traditional religious grounding obsolete. But with the obsolescence of religion, globalization, however inadvertently, undercuts the very prerequisite to a sustainable social order. Because of its inherent secularity, scholars are recognizing that globalization lacks the sacred by which a social order can be established, maintained, and perpetuated

---

[11] Emile Durkheim, *The Elementary Forms of the Religious Life*, trans. by Joseph Ward Swain (London: George Allen & Unwin Ltd., 1954), 7.

[12] Stjepan G. Meštrović, *Anthony Giddens: The Last Modernist* (London/New York: Routledge, 1998), 97.

[13] Giddens, *Runaway World*, 61-65, 91.

which, as in the case with its demographic contradictions above, is significantly threatening the very survival of entire populations.[14] Thus, a number of nations have begun the intentional process of returning to their religious roots as a way of overcoming globalization's social deficiencies and restoring their own future civilizational flourishing.[15]

******

In what follows, I will explore these twin developments of demographic and political responses to globalization and how they are radically altering our world towards a pronounced Christian majority. In Part I, we'll explore the particulars of a massive demographic revolution going on in the West, where a significant fertility discrepancy between conservative religionists and their secular counterparts promises a far more religious and religiously conservative future. In Part II, we'll look at how this demographic discrepancy appears to be already evidencing itself in the surge of Christian commitment and self-identity in both the United States and Europe. Then, in Part III, we'll look at four case studies of how politics is currently being reshaped by the rise of Christian nationalism. Poland, Georgia, Hungary, and Russia each provide unique and dynamic examples of what such demographic and political paradigm shifts entail for the present, thus foreshadowing the hope of a far more religiously conservative future.

---

[14] Meštrović, *Giddens*, 151.
[15] See, for example, Monica Duffy Toft, Daniel Philpott, Timothy Samuel Shah, *God's Century: Resurgent Religion and Global Politics* (New York: Norton and Company, 2011).

PART I

THE DEMOGRAPHIC REVOLUTION

CHAPTER 1

Will the Modernists Inherit the Earth? The Dismal Demographics of Secular Liberalism

In view of the previously mentioned victory laps taken so frequently by secular liberals, the noted laments of many prominent conservatives of course starkly contrast the exuberant elation of many in the so-called mainstream media. As a large majority of pundits and journalists share an affinity with leftwing lifestyle values, such victory laps signify the wave of the future. When the first openly gay football player, Michael Sam, was drafted into the National Football League, Christine Brennan of USA Today hailed Sam as the most important football player in the nation, while Cyd Zeigler in Time argued that history would look back at his drafting as that moment when professional sports changed forever. And not to be outdone, the newly crowned Eurovision diva, a bearded transvestite, declared to the world: "This night is dedicated to everyone who believes in a future of peace and freedom. You know who you are! We are unity, and we are unstoppable!"

However, there are several significant indicators brewing under the surface that demur dramatically from such triumphalist prognostications, suggesting a considerable gap between the rhetoric and the reality; the future, as it turns out, is actually rather dire for secular liberalism.

According to University of London scholar Eric Kaufmann's detailed study on global demographic trends, we are in the early stages of nothing less than a demographic revolution. In Kaufmann's words, "religious fundamentalists are on course to take over the world."[16] There is a significant demographic deficit between secularists and conservative religionists. For example, in the U.S., while self-identified non-religionist women averaged only 1.5 children per couple in 2002, conservative evangelical women averaged 2.5 children, representing a 28 percent fertility edge. Kaufmann notes that this demographic deficit will have dramatic effects over time. In a population evenly divided, these numbers indicate that conservative evangelicals would increase from 50 to 62.5 percent of the population in a single generation. In two generations, their number would increase to 73.5 percent, and over the course of 200 years, they would represent 99.4 percent!

The Amish and Mormons provide contemporary illustrations of the compound effect of endogamous growth. The Amish double in population every twenty years, and projections have the Amish numbering over a million in the U.S. and Canada in just a few decades. Since 1830, Mormon growth has averaged 40 percent per decade, which means that by 2080, there may be as many as 267 million Mormons in the world, making them by 2100 anywhere from 1 to 6 percent of the world's population.

One explanation for this demographic revolution is a social phenomenon known as *retraditionalization.* or a renewed interest in "traditions of wisdom that have proved their validity through

---

[16] Kaufmann, Shall the Religious, ix.

the test of history," or "a longing for spiritual traditions and practices that have stood the test of time, and, therefore, can be valued as authentic resources for spiritual renewal."[17] The important point here is that retraditionalization is not limited simply to spiritual renewal or religious revival; it often involves a reconfiguration of political, cultural, and educational norms around pre-modern religious beliefs and practices as a response to the secularizing processes of globalization.[18] One study, in particular, found that retraditionalization largely explained the rise of fertility among ethnic enclaves in the nation of Kyrgyzstan, where the researchers found that the more such minorities felt threatened by the cultural pressures of the wider ethnic majority, the more they turned to procreation and fertility as the primary means of resisting such pressures.[19]

However, within secular globalist societies, retraditionalized families will not remain as enclaves for very long. In contrast to the flourishing fertility among conservative Christian families, Kaufmann's data projects that secularists, who consistently exemplify a low fertility rate of around 1.5 (significantly below the replacement level of 2.1), will begin a steady decline after 2030 to a mere 14 to 15 percent of the American population. Kaufmann thus appears to have identified what he calls "the soft underbelly of secularism," namely demography.[20] This is because secular liberalism entails its own "demographic contradiction," the affirmation of the sovereign individual devoid of the restraints of classical moral structures necessitates the freedom not to reproduce. The link between sex and procreation having

---

[17] Leif Gunnar Engedal, *"Homo Viator.* The Search for Identity and Authentic Spirituality in a Post-modern Context," in Kirsi Tirri (ed.) *Religion, Spirituality and Identity* (Bern: Peter Lang, 2006), 45-64, 58.
[18] Ivan Varga, "Detraditionalization and Retraditionalization," in Mark Juergensmeyer and Wade Clark Roof (eds.), *Encyclopedia of Global Religion* (Los Angeles: Sage Publications, 2012), 295-98, 297.
[19] Michele E. Commercio, "The Politics and Economics of 'Retraditionalization' in Kyrgyzstan and Tajikistan," *Post-Soviet Affairs* 31 no. 6 (2015): 529-56.
[20] Kaufmann, *Shall the Religious*, xv.

been broken, modernist reproduction translates into mere personal preference. It thus turns out that radical individualism, so celebrated and revered by contemporary secular propagandists, is, in fact, the agent by which their ideology implodes.

In Europe, immigration is ironically making the continent more religiously conservative, not less; in fact, London and Paris are some of the most religiously dense areas within their respective populations. In Britain, for example, Ultra-Orthodox or Haredi Jews constitute only 17 percent of the Jewish population but account for 75 percent of Jewish births. And in Israel, Haredi schoolchildren have gone from comprising a few percent to nearly a third of all Jewish pupils in a matter of five decades and are poised to represent the majority of the Jewish population by 2050. Since 1970, charismatic Christians in Europe have expanded steadily at a rate of 4 percent per year, in step with Muslim growth. Currently, Laestadian Lutherans in Finland and Holland's Orthodox Calvinists have a fertility advantage over their wider secular populations of 4:1 and 2:1 respectively.

Now, some may think that mass conversions can compensate for this demographic deficit, enticing the children of religious conservatives to break away and join the ranks of the secular. However, this is highly unlikely. The more conservative and vibrant the religious commitment, the more incentives there are for the next generations to remain faithful and concomitantly strong disincentives to leave. Indeed, we have statistics that demonstrate that children growing up in conservative religionist households are highly likely to maintain such conservative religious sentiments into their adult years. We also have studies that show that liberal religionists are more likely to become conservative than the other way around.[21] Thus, with clearly delineated social boundaries and identity markers, conservative endogamous groups are generally very difficult to break up. And Kaufmann's data suggests that the more conservative the group, the greater the demographic discrepancy as compared with secularist procreation.

Phillip Longman of ForeignPolicy.com has come to the same conclusion as Kaufmann and others. In a recently published article on the rising birthrates among conservatives in Europe and the United States, Longman notes that liberal critics of the traditional family are actually plagued by a rather inconvenient fact that the feminist and countercultural movements of the 1960s and 70s have not and are not leaving any genetic legacy. While only 11 percent of baby boomer women had four or more children, they made up over 25 percent of the total children born to baby boomers. Conversely, the 20 percent of women who had only one child accounted for a mere 7 percent of the total children born to baby boomers. Specifically, he cites statistics from France, where only about 30 percent of women have three or more children, but they're responsible for over 50 percent of all French births.

Thus, Longman concludes that this fertility discrepancy is "leading to the emergence of a new society whose members will disproportionately be descended from parents who rejected the social tendencies that once made childlessness and small families the norm. These values include adherence to traditional, patriarchal religion, and a strong identification with one's own folk or nation."[22]

---

[21] Stark, *Triumph*, 188, 191, 194.
[22] https://foreignpolicy.com/2009/10/20/the-return-of-patriarchy/.

Now, Longman notes that this demographic dynamic helps explain, for example, what he calls the gradual shift of American culture away from secular individualism and towards what he calls "religious fundamentalism," or what I would prefer, religious traditionalism. He notes that among states that voted for President George W. Bush in 2004, the fertility rates in those states were 12 percent higher than in states that voted for Sen. John Kerry. Turning his attention across the pond, Longman notes that this demographic discrepancy may account, at least partially, for why Europeans are beginning more and more to reject what he calls the crown jewel of secular liberalism, the European Union. And this is because, as it turns out, those Europeans who are most likely to identify themselves as "world citizens" and globalists are also those least likely to have children. Longman cites demographic data that found that those with globalist values, those who had a high enthusiasm for alternative lifestyles and a marked complacency towards cultural traditions and customs, were far less likely to get married and have kids than those who exemplified more nationalist sentiments, such as a deep reverence for nation, culture, custom, and tradition. And so, in Europe and the States, we're finding that the number of children different people have, and under what circumstances, actually correlates very strongly with their beliefs on a wide range of political and cultural attitudes.

We may be seeing a further indicator of this demographic revolution. According to a recent Gallup poll that asked, "What do you think is the ideal number of children for a family to have?" More Americans than at any point since the early 1970s said they considered three or more children as the ideal size of the family.[23]

---

[23] https://www.cnsnews.com/news/article/natalia-mittelstadt/poll-41-say-families-3-or-more-children-ideal-34-2011.

According to the poll, 41 percent said they wanted three or more children, which is up from 34 percent back in 2011. Moreover, the same poll found that those who believed that 4 or more children to be ideal also increased from 9 percent in 2007 to 15 percent in 2018. Gallup has been tracking this question each year for the last several decades, and they found that between the years of 1967 and 1971, attitudes towards the family have changed dramatically. The percentage that wanted a large family fell from 70 percent down to around 50 percent, a 20-point drop, corresponding to the height of the widespread fear concerning overpopulation in the late 1960s and early 1970s. Such sentiments fell to an all-time low in 1986, when only 26 percent of those polled wanted a big family.

But there's little question that the last several years have seen a noticeable trend towards a renewed popularity for relatively big families, consisting of 3 or more children. And what's particularly interesting here is that the current average ideal is around 2.7 children per couple, up from 2.5 in 2007 and then again in 2011. Note how this corresponds with Kaufmann's statistic regarding conservative Christian populations in the US, who are averaging 2.5 children per couple, which is significantly above the 2.1 replacement threshold. So, the Gallup poll is averaging out at around the same size of the average conservative family found in Kaufmann's studies. We may thus be seeing the beginnings of the transition from a secular globalist conception of the family with very low birth rates to a conservative traditionalist conception of the family with its comparably high birth rates.

And so, the rhetoric of the secular modernist predicting the inexorable global triumph of the sovereign individual seems little more than a chimera, a pipe dream that is itself the product of self-centered aspirations and ambitions. The reality is that demographic trends suggest that the dominance of secular liberalism is, in fact, on the verge of collapse. It does appear that religious conservatives, not secular liberals, will inherit the world after all.

CHAPTER 2

Europe and the Nationalist Baby Boom

Our discovery of the demographic revolution currently underway among conservative religionists is by no means limited to contemporary enclaves within Western nations. A number of governments are bolstering such a revolution by promoting pro-life and pro-family domestic policies aimed specifically at reversing their falling birth rates for the purpose of revitalizing their national culture and character. There are four nations in particular that we shall survey: Hungary, Poland, Russia, and Georgia. Each of these nations has implemented specific pro life policies that are effectively reversing their populations decline into one of significant increase. We'll then look at the logical connection between a revived sense of nationalism and renewed pro-family sentiments, a connection that promises to see the continuation of increased fertility in the years ahead.

As we explored above, few would disagree that there is, in fact, a rampant demographic decline plaguing Europe over the last several years, particularly as a result of falling birth rates. Projections are rather dire: the UN Population Division predicted that Europe could lose as many as 100 million people in the next 50 years, representing nearly 20 percent of its population. *The*

Economist magazine recently ran an article declaring, somewhat predictably, that this fertility freefall is precisely why Europe needs immigrants. After all, so we are told, if Europeans are going to maintain the integrity of their welfare policies, especially for the elderly, they will have to compensate for the inevitable loss of manpower and tax revenue with significant immigration rates.

And yet, what appears to have escaped the myopic gaze of the editors of *The Economist* is the fact that a number of European nations, those particularly with nationalist populist governments, have been demonstrating that there's a further option for resolving this demographic decline: *the revitalization of the traditional family.* We now have data indicating that a number of intentional efforts to promote and perpetuate the traditional family are, in fact, producing significant reversals in fertility deficits.

For example, in Hungary, the government of Prime Minister Viktor Orban implemented two major pro-family reforms. First, in 2011, the parliament adopted a new constitution which states explicitly that "We believe that our children and grandchildren will make Hungary great again," and which defends "the institution of marriage as the union of a man and a woman... and the family as the basis of the nation's survival."[24] Secondly, the government instituted a policy back in 2015 called the 'Family Housing Allowance Program' that gave very generous subsidies to buy or build new homes based on the number of children the couple had. To qualify, couples had to have three or more children, at least for the top tier benefits, which consisted of the equivalent of a $36,000 grant to buy a new home, along with generous tax breaks as well. By some estimates, families with

---

[24] Victoria Friedman, "Make Babies Great Again: Hungarian Fertility Rates Rise, Turns Back Demographic Decline," https://www.breitbart.com/europe/2018/07/12/hungary-sees-rising-fertility-rate-turns-back-demographic-decline/.

several children could receive upwards of $60,000 in subsidies and tax credits.[25] As a result of these cultural and financial incentives, Hungary's birthrate has been steadily increasing from 2010, placing it just behind France and Austria in terms of the highest birthrates in Europe.

So, too, in Poland, a nation that has also been implementing pro-family measures, which are effectively reversing Poland's alarming demographic decline over the last several years. As of 2015, Poland's birth rate was 1.32 children per woman; only Portugal had a lower fertility rate.[26] So, in 2015, the nationalist right-wing Law and Justice Party instituted a plan to give 500 zlotys ($150) each month to each family for every child they had after their first.[27] Such measures, along with Poland's thoroughly pro-life abortion restrictions, appear to have contributed to a trend that started just before these measures, where Poland's fertility has increased from 1.29 children per woman in 2012 to nearly 1.5 in 2016. While still below the replacement rate of 2.1, this increase means that Poland has gone from one of the lowest birthrates in Europe to one of the highest. Poles were in twentieth place among European repopulation statistics in 2015; today, Poland ranks just behind Hungary.

Another example of a dramatic demographic reversal is the Russian Federation. When President Vladimir Putin assumed office, Russia was losing people on average of almost a million a year.[28] Moreover, Russia had one of the highest abortion rates in the world, an apparent hangover from the Soviet Union being the first state in the world to legalize abortion. In fact, one scholar estimated that

[25] Lyman Stone, "Is Hungary Experiencing a Policy-Induced Baby Boom?" https://ifstudies.org/blog/is-hungary-experiencing-a-policy-induced-baby-boom.
[26] https://www.theguardian.com/world/2017/nov/09/breed-like-rabbits-and-reverse-population-decline-poles-urged.
[27] https://www.mercatornet.com/demography/view/the-polish-fertility-rise/21126.
[28] https://www.theguardian.com/world/2015/may/06/vladimir-putin-15-ways-he-changed-russia-world.

termination rates in Russian rural areas were as high as 770 abortions per 100 births in 1985.[29] However, President Putin enacted a number of policies to reverse these population-declining trends, such as the banning of abortion advertising and banning abortion after 12 weeks of pregnancy. Moreover, the Russian Orthodox Church instituted efforts to set up social support for the family, such as support centers for pregnant women in difficult situations (something akin to crisis pregnancy centers in the US), while promoting the development of education on the dangers of abortions. There is thus little coincidence that Russia has experienced a 20 percent increase in births over the course of the last few years; in fact, 2015 was the first year that Russia experienced an increase of births since the fall of the Soviet Union. Moreover, Russians are treated to an annual ceremony at the Kremlin where Vladimir Putin himself publicly honors families that have upwards of eight or more children, what we might call 'super families,' as symbols of a flourishing future for Russia.

We've also seen extraordinary success surrounding the Georgian Orthodox Church's campaign to revitalize the family. For a number of years, Georgia has had one of the lowest birthrates in Eastern Europe. And so, back in 2008, Patriarch Ilia II began a campaign where he promised to personally baptize the third or higher child of married Orthodox couples. Since then, to the astonishment of demographers, Georgia has gone from having one of the lowest birthrates in Eastern Europe to now actually one of the highest.[30]

---

[29] Vyacheslav Karpov and Kimmo Kääriänen, "'Abortion Culture' in Russia: Its Origins, Scope, and Challenge to Social Development," *Journal of Applied Sociology*, Vol. 22, No. 2 (Fall-Winter 2005-06): 13-33.
[30] https://ifstudies.org/blog/in-georgia-a-religiously-inspired-baby-boom.

Now, these recent baby booms confirm studies that have been done on the relationship between nationalism and pro-family sentiments.[31] What these studies found was that nationalist movements tend to accompany resurgent birthrates among populations, since nationalist sentiments take the health and perpetuation of a people and their culture, customs, and traditions very seriously. Think, for example, of the movie *My Big Fat Greek Wedding*. If you haven't seen the film, there's a young Greek woman named Tula who has this large, proud, nationalist Greek family who lives in Chicago. To the shock of everyone, she gets engaged to this 'regular American' named Ian Miller, who she'd been secretly dating for several weeks. Ian Miller comes from a typical American secular family. And so, on the day of their wedding, the father walks his daughter down the aisle of the Greek Orthodox Church while the camera-scene pans over the entire sanctuary. What's unmistakable to the viewer is that we can see on Ian Miller's family's side, the secular side as it were, just a handful of family members in attendance, while the right side, the bride's side, is utterly filled with Tula's family members. And here you can see the contrast between a religious, nationalist, traditionalist vision of the family and this blatantly dissipating secular view of the family, a rather astonishing commentary, however inadvertent, on the social differences between secular and traditionalist conceptions of fertility and demography.

Nationalist, populist, and traditionalist societies see the family as indispensable to the perpetuation of the nation, culture, and customs that make us truly human, and thus the family is seen not as a mere lifestyle choice, so prevalent among secular globalists, but indeed the prerequisite for a humane and flourishing life. It is,

---

[31] P. Albanese, "Abortion and reproductive rights under nationalist regimes in twentieth-century Europe," *Women's Health and Urban Life* 3 (1) (2004): 8-33.

therefore, not surprising to discover, as we found above, that conservative religionists consistently exemplify very high birthrates, as in the approximate 2.5 children per couple in the US, which is significantly higher than the 2.1 replacement rate. And given that nationalist movements entail a process that scholars call *retraditionalization*, which is the re-embracing, the renewal and revival of a nation's customs, culture, and traditions, it's no coincidence that the new nationalist movements in places like Hungary, Poland, Russia, and Georgia are experiencing the revival of the traditional family.

And so, as it turns out, nationalist populists are having children while secular globalists are not. I think we can, therefore, peer into the future here as we are, in fact, seeing these nations leading the way to a demographic renewal that will impact the European continent for generations to come.

PART II

CHRISTENDOM RISING

CHAPTER 3

The Renewal of American Conservative Christianity

For most of the twentieth-century, sociologists have advocated a concept known as the 'secularization thesis.'[32] The secularization thesis was popularized by sociologists such as Emile Durkheim and Max Weber, who argued that religious ideas, institutions, and interpretations would inevitably wane in terms of their social importance as societies became more technological and industrial. Sociologists believed they were observing a correlation between the level of education and technology characterizing a society and its religious commitment; of course, it was a contrary correlation: the more educated and technological our societies get, the less religious they'll be. Western sociologists related the secularization thesis primarily to Christianity; proponents of secularization postulated that a combination of younger generations and higher education would basically wipe out historic Christianity.

The secularization thesis was, in fact, the dominant religious paradigm in sociology for most of the twentieth century. And we still

---

[32] See, for example, Dylan Reaves, "Peter Berger and the Rise and Fall of the Theory of Secularization," https://digitalcommons.denison.edu/cgi/viewcontent.cgi?article=1076&context=religion.

hear it today; many continue to claim that science and religion have nothing to do with each other, or that the more educated a person is, the less likely they are to be a religious fanatic.

And yet, a recent study by scholars from Harvard University and Indiana University Bloomington provides a stark challenge to such a thesis. Published in the Journal of Sociological Science under the title, "The Persistent and Exceptional Intensity of American Religion: A Response to Recent Research," researchers compiled data on the state of American Christianity that thoroughly refutes the secularization thesis.[33] What makes this study so interesting is that they use a metric that they call 'level of intensity' in one's various religious commitments and practices, such as a literalist commitment to Scripture as the authoritative Word of God, the frequency of church attendance, and their propensity towards evangelism. What this means is that this study can make a distinction between what we would call 'conservative or traditionalist Christianity' on the one hand and 'liberal or modernist Christianity' on the other, and the findings here are very interesting.

What the study concluded was that the percentage of the American population who attend church one or more times a week, who pray daily, and who accept the Bible as the inspired Word of God has remained relatively unchanged for the last 50 years. And given the population increase during that time period, the percentage of conservative Christians has risen proportionately to the rise in the American population in general. This observation was corroborated earlier by studies compiled by sociologist Rodney Stark, who noted that since 1980, church attendance has remained constant.[34] But as such researchers have

[33] https://www.sociologicalscience.com/download/vol-4/november/SocSci_v4_686to700.pdf.
[34] Stark, *Triumph*, 188-92.

noted, this raises a rather significant question for sociological theory: if committed church attendance has not decreased in any identifiable manner over the last several decades, then where precisely is this rising secularism that sociologists have thus far told us about? If the percentage of Americans who attend church regularly and receive the Bible as the inspired Word of God has not changed in the least, then by definition neither has the percentage of the population that sees itself as secular.

As Rodney Stark notes, a glaring error made by several media outlets is to equate the rising number of self-declared 'nones' – those who don't associate with any religion – with a rising rate of secular sensibilities. The important point that Stark makes is that the data shows that this rise of self-affiliated 'nones' hasn't affected the actual percentage of the population that regularly attends church. So whatever change is taking place in terms of self-designation, it's taking place *within* an already non-church attending group, *and this group has not grown.* And so, what we're finding is that pollsters simply invented a new term such as 'nones,' and more people that were already part of the non-church attending population found that they associated better with that term. The conclusion is inescapable: secularists are simply not rising as a percentage of the population in the US. In fact, more Americans now belong to a local church than ever before.

Now the Harvard study goes on to point out that these church-attendance percentages are hardly peripheral in American life: one in three Americans prays multiple times a day, and one-third of Americans hold that the Bible is the actual word of God. By contrast, these numbers are generally less than 10 percent in European countries, for example. And so, these scholars conclude that the United States "clearly stands out as exceptional" in its religious commitments, and this exceptionalism has not decreased in any measurable way over the last several decades. In fact, researchers suggest that the percentage may actually be increasing.

Now, as I alluded above, what's also so illuminating here is that this study examines how American religion is also being restructured around conservative and liberal lines. What they found was that the liberal mainline churches were quite literally hemorrhaging members. Take the ultra-liberal Presbyterian Church USA for example. The PCUSA has been imploding in terms of membership for years. They lost nearly 100,000 members in 2014. They were nearly half a million short from their numbers just three years ago, where they were at about two million, and they're on track to lose another half a million by 2020. Or take the United Methodist Church; it's lost hundreds of thousands of members. In fact, their membership loss of late has been equated to them losing the equivalent of a 300-member local parish per day! And the loss appears to be compounded; the actual percentage of membership loss in the United Methodist Church is actually increasing, so while they might have seen a 1 percent drop in membership in 2013, they're seeing a 2 percent drop in 2014.

Now, by contrast, conservative, particularly evangelical churches, are growing significantly. What's happening is that conservative evangelicals are becoming a markedly larger proportion of all religious people in the US. In 1989, almost 40 percent of the total aggregate of those who belonged to a religion held what these scholars called intense beliefs and practices. Today, it's nearly 50 percent of all the religiously affiliated. And as Glenn Stanton over at the Federalist noted, this increase in the percentage of conservative evangelicals among America's religious population has important implications for politics since it means that the voting bloc of religious conservatives is not shrinking but is actually growing stronger.[35] So much for the waning influence of the Religious Right that we keep hearing about.

The irony to all of this *is* a kind of confirmation of the secularization thesis in our midst, but it appears specific and peculiar to a particular demographic, namely populations prone to adopting as normative liberal and modernist visions of life. They appear to have lost the capacity to sustain and perpetuate distinctive Christian beliefs and practices, whereas those who are committed to conservative and traditionalist values appear to provide the social frames of reference whereby historical Christian beliefs and practices flourish, thus accounting for the steady church attendance numbers.

This realignment of religion around conservative vs. liberal sensibilities was first recognized by Robert Wuthnow in his 1988 study entitled *The Restructuring of American Religion*. Wuthnow argues that since World War II, American religiosity has been going through a re-alignment away from doctrinal distinctives and instead, around political and cultural values. While denominational and doctrinal issues were key identifying markers prior to World War II, Americans have been increasingly defining themselves as conservatives or liberals. Thus, a conservative Episcopalian will find that he has more in common with a conservative Catholic or even a conservative Mormon than he does with a fellow Episcopalian who happens to be a liberal progressive. The important point here is that United States really is going through a mass realignment along liberal globalist vs.

---

[35] Glenn T. Stanton, "New Harvard Research Says U.S. Christianity Is Not Shrinking, But Growing Stronger," https://www.sociologicalscience.com/download/vol-4/november/SocSci_v4_686to700.pdf

conservative traditionalist lines. This latest Harvard-Indiana University study is but the latest set of data to indicate just that.

The question is then: what if these trends continue, as the last several decades suggest that they will? Does it not follow that the 40 percent aggregate of Americans regularly attending church will go from being comprised of a 50-50 conservative/liberal ratio to a 75-25 ratio in a matter of a couple of decades? How long before it becomes a 90-10 split? What are the political and cultural ramifications for a nation when 40 percent of its population is theologically and socially conservative Christians? At the very least, we can surmise that the whole contemporary notion that the world is becoming more secular, more progressive, more liberal, would be itself ironically consigned to the ash heap of history.

It does appear that the latest research confirms and corroborates what we have already been observing in terms of the demographic and fertility data. If the sociology of the American church is at least subtly exemplative of larger social trends, secular modernist liberalism is indeed waning, and in its place, a new religiously conservative age is rising.

CHAPTER 4

A New Christendom?
The Revival of Christianity in Europe

A re we seeing the beginnings of a Christian revival in
Europe? That's what John D. Martin over at *The Federalist*
believes, and he makes quite a good argument for it.[36]
His excellent article reveals what appears to be a rather sustained
revival or renaissance of Christian-themed enthusiasm in Europe,
a renewal which is hardly reported on at all and barely noticed by
the European press. But it appears to be very real and very
impressive.

He begins first with Spain, where he cites a 2014 study that found
a very significant increase in the percentage of Spaniards who
were attending Catholic Mass; church attendance rose from 12
percent in 2011 to 15 percent in the following year, 2012. But even
more impressive, between 2012 and 2013, church attendance
grew by an astonishing 23 percent; and when you look at the
numbers of Spaniards who voluntarily support the church through
their taxes, those numbers rose by over a million between 2007

---

[36] http://thefederalist.com/2018/03/23/reports-christianitys-death-europe-greatly-exaggerated/.

and 2013. So, church attendance and participation are on a very significant uptick in Spain.

A comparably encouraging picture comes from France. Of interest is the recent increase in men participating in vocational calls to the priesthood and religious life in the various Catholic orders. But it's not just the Catholic Church that's seeing signs of growth; we're seeing the rise of evangelical churches in traditionally Catholic France as well; in fact, statistics show that a new evangelical church opens every 10 days in France. Moreover, over 30 French evangelical churches have congregations of 1,000 or more. Just in the last 60 years, the number of Evangelical Protestants has increased tenfold.

In Germany, 2016 statistics indicate that the Evangelical Church received nearly 200,000 new members in that year alone. And when charismatic and Pentecostal numbers are included, the German Protestant church grew 6 percent over the last two years. John Martin's analysis of church growth in Germany cites an annual national conference that corroborates these growing numbers. The 2018 Mehr Conference (Mehr meaning 'More' as in 'More of Christ') drew more than 11,000 attendees, which is a 100-fold increase from the first conference held back in 2008. Of significance here is the appeal this revived Christianity has for the young; when the moderators at the last conference asked everyone in the audience who were younger than 22 to stand, it was reported that nearly *half* of the 11,000 in attendance stood up. We're seeing comparable enthusiasm with events like "Awakening Europe" where tens of thousands of young people gather together to worship and hear evangelistic preaching; the latest one in Prague saw over a thousand young people commit their lives to Christ for the very first time. A similar event with mass numbers of conversions happened in Stockholm, Sweden as well. It thus appears that the whole notion that the European church is an aging, dying church actually just doesn't fit the actual demographics of church attendees.

He then jumps over to Eastern Europe and again cites reports of a Christian revival going on in Viktor Orban's Hungary, as well as the massive surge in church attendance in Poland, which exceeds, if you can believe it, 40 percent of the population. Over in Russia, a number of studies corroborate that there is nothing less than an extraordinary Christian revival going on in the former Soviet Union.[37] For example, in 1991, only 37 percent of Russians identified as Orthodox Christians. Now that number has risen to over 70 percent. And it's not just Russia; in 1991, only 39 percent of Ukrainians identified as Orthodox Christians; today it is 80 percent. And back in the 1990s, about 60 percent of Bulgarians identified as Orthodox Christians; today it is 75 percent. And a number of surveys found that over 90 percent of people in Greece, Romania, Moldova, Armenia, and Georgia all said they believe in God and affirm a Christian identity. Pew Research Center found comparable numbers when they recently surveyed 15 countries in Western Europe. When asked to identify one's religion if any, the vast majority of Western Europeans still identify themselves as Christians. For example, over 70 percent of Germans identified as Christian, 80 percent of Austrians, 80 percent of Italians, nearly 80 percent of Fins, and 65 percent of Danes.[38]

Now, it's at this point that studies tend to turn somewhat skeptical, noting that though a significant percentage of Europeans identify themselves as Christians, very few regularly attend church. This is

---

[37] See, for example, Geoffrey Evans and Ksenia Northmore-Ball, "The Limits of Secularization? The Resurgence of Orthodoxy in Post-Soviet Russia," *Journal for the Scientific Study of Religion* Vol. 51, Is. 4 (December 2012): 795-808.
[38] http://www.pewforum.org/2018/05/29/being-christian-in-western-europe/.

why Pew Research suggests that Europe remains Christian in name only; in reality, Europeans remain very, very secular. But here I think Pew and others are being a bit careless; and this is because when it comes to European religious piety, especially when we cite these statistics that show that the percentage of the European population that attends church is relatively low, what we overlook is that Europeans *have always been characterized by rather sparse church attendance.* Even at the height of the medieval theocratic period, the churches were primarily located in the cities while most of the population lived in rural villages. Rodney Stark documents first-hand accounts from bishops no less, corroborating that the vast majority of the medieval European population did not attend church on any regular basis.[39] And yet, medieval were a thoroughly religious, Christian people; they certainly considered themselves Christians and citizens of Christendom; they firmly believed in God, angels, demons, heaven, hell, and divinely enforced moral accountability. But the irony here is that because they didn't attend church, Pew research – if it were to be consistent – would have counted your average medieval villager every bit as secular as they designate the modern European!

Instead of focusing church attendance rates as the sole indicator of Christian commitment, a 2012 study in the *Journal for the Scientific Study of Religion* examined the question as to whether Russia was experiencing a genuine religious revival. The study used a number of criteria for analyzing the occurrence of just such a revival, such as the age and educational levels of professed believers, church attendance, and commitment to traditional moral values. These manifold criteria produced illuminative results. For example, in terms of age and educational levels, the

---

[39] Stark, *Triumph*, 41-44.

study found that the Russians most likely to identify as Orthodox Christian were of the younger generation and represented all levels across the educational spectrum. The reason why this is important – the age and educational levels – is that it amounts to a total repudiation of the secularization hypothesis that was so dominant in the social sciences over the last century, which postulated that a combination of younger generations and higher education would basically wipe out historic Christianity. And yet, Russia was seeing growth in Christian identity and commitment among the young and highly educated.

Another indicator of Christian identity is the level of commitment to traditional moral values. And here the Pew survey is quite revealing. An average of 85 percent of Orthodox Christians among all the countries surveyed believed homosexual behavior to be morally wrong. This includes Armenia, Moldova, Georgia, Belarus, Russia, Ukraine, Romania, Serbia, Bulgaria, and Greece. The Armenians ranked first with 98 percent of their population affirming the sinfulness of homosexual behavior and lifestyle, while Greece was last with only 51 percent affirming such.[40]

Moreover, research is showing mass support of church-state cooperation in Eastern Europe. The Pew Survey found very strong support for President Vladimir Putin as well as the Moscow Patriarch Kirill over the Constantinopolitan Patriarch Bartholomew, who's seen as more or less just a puppet of the secular West. Both President Putin and Patriarch Kirill are seen as defenders of traditional Orthodox civilization against the anti-cultural, anti-traditional tendencies in the liberal globalization of the secular West. The survey found that a vast majority of the populations in Eastern Europe supported the state funding the church and

---

[40] http://www.pewforum.org/2018/10/29/eastern-and-western-europeans-differ-on-importance-of-religion-views-of-minorities-and-key-social-issues/

Christian missions and spreading Christian civilization throughout the world.

And it's not just Eastern Europe that's exemplifying political sentiments distinctive of Christian identity. Pew found that self-professed Christians in Western Europe, both church-going and non-church-going, were far more likely to oppose immigration and are far more likely to see Islam as incompatible with European culture and values than their non-religionist counterparts. So, for example, in the UK, 45% of church-attending Christians say Islam is fundamentally incompatible with British values and culture, as do 47% of non-church-attending Christians. Said differently, nearly 50 percent of self-identified Christians – which represents 73 percent of the British population – see Islam as fundamentally incompatible with British culture and values. By contrast, among those who remain religiously unaffiliated, only about 30 percent said that Islam is fundamentally incompatible with their country's values. So, there's a clear differentiation between self-identified Christians and the religiously unaffiliated when it comes to more nationalist and populist sentiments.

Similar numbers appear elsewhere; in Angela Merkel's Germany, 55% of churchgoing Christians and 45% of non-practicing Christians agree that Islam is incompatible with German values. In Austria, it's over 60 percent. In Italy, more than half of both practicing and non-practicing Christians see Islam as completely incompatible with their national culture and values, and in Finland, it was nearly 70 percent. Indeed, we've further found that more than half of Finns believe that it is very important to have been born and have ancestry in a country to truly share its national identity.

The question remains: what accounts for why are we seeing such a significant commitment to Christian identity across the continent?

In my book, *The Triumph of Tradition*, I made the extended argument that the current resurgence of religion can be attributed to a phenomenon known as *retraditionalization*, a renewed interest in "traditions of wisdom that have proved their validity through the test of history," or "a longing for spiritual traditions and practices that have stood the test of time, and, therefore, can be valued as authentic resources for spiritual renewal."[41] The important point here is that retraditionalization is not limited simply to spiritual renewal or religious revival; it often involves a reconfiguration of political, cultural, and educational norms around pre-modern religious beliefs and practices as a response to the secularizing processes of globalization.[42] In the face of threats to a sense of place, identity, and security, populations tend to reassert historic identity and security markers, such as religion, custom, and tradition as mechanisms of resistance against secular globalization's anti-cultural, anti-traditional dynamics. Or in Kinnvall's words: "As individuals feel vulnerable and experience existential anxiety, it is not uncommon for them to wish to reaffirm a threatened self-identity. Any collective identity that can provide such security is a potential pole of attraction."[43]

And so, as Europe is currently experiencing a surge of nationalist populism throughout its member nations, what many scholars often overlook is that an essential part of that nationalism and populism is a retraditionalization that provides the spiritual roots that serve to revitalize and sustain the resurgence of nationalist

---

[41] Engedal, *"Homo Viator,"* 45-64, 58.
[42] Ivan Varga, "Detraditionalization and Retraditionalization," in Mark Juergensmeyer and Wade Clark Roof (eds.), *Encyclopedia of Global Religion* (Los Angeles: Sage Publications, 2012), 295-98, 297.
[43] Catarina Kinnvall, "Globalization and Religious Nationalism: Self, Identity, and the Search for Ontological Security," *Political Psychology* Vol. 25, No. 5 (Oct, 2004): 741-767, 742.

populism. And I would argue that this is precisely what we are seeing in Europe; it really does appear that we are seeing nothing less than a mass religious awakening, indeed a Christian revival going on throughout Europe that is beginning to effectively counter the secularizing globalism that has dominated the continent since the end of the second world war. The appears to be an abundance of evidence for a dramatic spiritual shift taking place in Europe toward the renewal and growth in each of the denominational expressions of Christianity, a spiritual shift that promises to reawaken a new conservative age in our midst.

PART III

THE NEW CHRISTIAN MAJORITY

CHAPTER 5

Poland and the National
Christian Renewal

I n June of 1979, the recently elected pope, John Paul II, passed through the Iron Curtain, back to his homeland of Poland. Over the course of nine days, the world witnessed a profound display of distinctly Christian hope, as John Paul II prayed in the presence of hundreds of thousands of Poles: "Let your Holy Spirit descend and renew the face of this earth and this land." Such prayers ignited the moral imaginations of a people bound under the yoke of communism and atheistic materialism, sparkling a mass movement of liberation that swept over Eastern Europe in the course of a decade. It was called the 'summer of hope.'

I couldn't help but think of that summer when I read about a ceremony at the Church of Divine Mercy in Krakow on November 19th, 2016, where the Catholic Bishops of Poland, in the presence of President Andrzej Duda and many Catholic pilgrims, officially recognized Jesus Christ as the King of Poland and called upon Him to rule over their nation, its people and their political leaders. It was as if those prayers of John Paul II were being fulfilled on that day; we were witnessing nothing short of the

Holy Spirit descending upon Poland awakening a model Christian civilization.

Church attendance, too, has been on the rise of late. According to figures from the Institute of Statistics of the Catholic Church in Poland, the percentage of people regularly attending church in Poland rose in 2015 from 39.1 percent to about 40 percent, which is a significant departure from the trend marking the decline in church attendance in many parts of Western Europe. According to the religion website Zenit.org, there was what they called a "massive" surge in church participation across the country: there were 369,000 baptisms, 360,000 confirmations, 270,000 first communions, and 134,000 marriages.[44] All of this was taking place on top of a study in 2014 that found that there were more than 60,000 parish organizations involving 2.5 million people active in Poland, along with nearly 2,000 Catholic social institutions such as schools or hospices. Furthermore, the number of Catholic priests in Poland also rose to a record 20,800, which as Breitbart news observes, suggests that Poland is rejecting the secular liberalism of institutions such as the European Union (EU) and embracing its traditional Christian culture.[45]

And Christianity is beginning to infuse every aspect of Polish political life. Recently, the Polish parliament proposed legislation that would have banned abortion from the nation. Poland already has one of the most restrictive laws in Europe, allowing for abortion in only three cases: rape, the risk of the life of the mother, and serious malformations in the fetus. While the proposed bill didn't pass, the Polish government continues to push for a new law that would be a near total ban. And in the face of tremendous pressure from eurocrats in the European Union

---

[44] https://zenit.org/articles/statistics-participation-at-sunday-mass-in-poland-has-risen-to-nearly-40/.
[45] https://www.breitbart.com/europe/2017/01/11/church-attendance-increases-conservative-poland/.

and NGOs to accept so-called 'same-sex marriage,' Poland has stood unmovable. Its constitution is one of seven in the European Union to ban same-sex marriage and is one of six that refuse to recognize same-sex civil unions.

Moreover, Poland has begun to protect its borders from mass immigration and the ensuing cultural upheaval that such immigration entails. In March of 2016, the Polish government announced that it would not accept 7,000 migrants that it had previously agreed to take under European Union pressure, and polls indicate that this is precisely the will of the vast majority of the Polish people. In October of 2017, thousands of Polish Catholics formed human chains on the nation's borders, praying that God would save Poland, Europe, and the world from Islamization. They recited their rosaries together as a mass spiritual force, and they were lined up along the 2,200-mile border with Germany, the Czech Republic, Slovakia, Ukraine, Belarus, Lithuania, Russia and the Baltic Sea. And even people in boats joined the event to help form chains across Polish rivers. During the mass that was held and which was broadcast live on television, the archbishop of Krakow called on believers to pray for all European nations that they may understand that it is necessary to return to their Christian roots so that Europe would remain Europe. Europe is a Christian land through and through.

The Polish government is even in the process of sanctifying time. The conservative-dominated parliament has also begun the process of abolishing shopping on Sundays with the express purpose to allow workers to spend more time with their families. The current law limits shopping on Sundays to the first and last Sunday of the month.[46] That will be followed by a further

---

[46] https://www.theguardian.com/world/2018/mar/11/poland-sunday-trading-ban-takes-effect.

reduction in the next year to shopping only on the last Sunday of the month, which is then followed by a total ban in the year 2020. Special allowances are, of course, granted for busy shopping periods, such as the run-up to Christmas or Easter or other holidays. But this latest effort by the Polish legislatures, I think is very significant in reconfiguring time and space around a renewed Christian conception of life

While the government's efforts to limit abortion, protect borders and sanctify Sundays are essential to maintaining Poland's Christian values, nothing replaces Poland's distinctive Catholic nationalism. While nationalism has the powerful effect of keeping people out who don't share Poland's Christian values, it is nevertheless wholly inclusive. Polish nationalism welcomes all peoples, races, and ethnicities to share in the blessings of Christian civilization, but only as long as they are willing to protect and perpetuate a common tradition, custom, and culture rooted in Christian ideals and practices.

What the current conservative Law and Justice Party recognizes is that borders and boundaries are essential to maintaining one's cultural and religious identity. Said differently, the problem when a nation opens up its borders akin to the open-border prescriptions of the European Union inevitably result in a proportionate openness of values. This certainly was the conclusion of the renowned social anthropologist Mary Douglas who developed the critical connection between borders and bodies in human culture.[47] She observed that cultural concerns about the body, such as taboo codes, ethical identity and conceptions of purity, are frequently lived out as metaphors for larger social relationships and boundaries. This term, *boundaries*, is a key motif for Douglas, who theorized that

---

[47] Mary Douglas, Purity and Danger: An Analysis of the Concepts of Pollution and Taboo (New York: Routledge, 2002 [1966]).

each individual body within the group 'body' shares in the boundedness of the group, such that the restrictions characteristic of the larger social order are embodied and reflected in each individual person. So, for example, restrictions as to whom one may betroth reflect restrictions as to who may enter the society; proscriptions protecting bodily orifices symbolize preoccupations about social exits and entrances. The do's and don'ts regulating national boundaries are lived out personally via the moral codes inscribed on individual bodies. If anyone can enter your country, well then, by definition, you can marry anyone. If there are no restrictions at your national border, there will be a comparable absence of restrictions in your personal and moral order.

So, if Douglas is correct, and I most certainly believe that she is, then there is a plausible cultural sense that *open borders mean open values*. The perpetuation of unfettered immigration fulfills the political precondition for more liberal democratic social policies. So, I believe that Poland is absolutely doing the right thing in protecting its borders against unfettered immigration since such protection involves the mutual protection of its Christian values and identity.

All of this is to say that we are indeed seeing the rise of a very confident, proud, and vibrant Christian Poland. Assuming a renewed leadership role, both moral and economic, in European civilization, Poland has become a bright example for the rest of the continent to follow in the renaissance of Christian civilization, a permanent emblem of the 'summer of hope.'

CHAPTER 6

The Postsecular Vision of
the Republic of Georgia

'Postsecular' is a term that scholars have coined as a descriptive means of explaining what's being called the 'return of religion,' or the resilience of religious traditions in modern life. As we noted above, for most of the twentieth century, social theorists generally believed that religion was supposed to disappear in the modern world; the more we advanced scientifically and technologically, the less religious we would be. But as even a cursory glance around the world reveals, religion didn't die out; with all the scientific and technological progress duly noted, religion stubbornly stuck around. In fact, not only is religion still here but in many ways, religion has only grown stronger and more prevalent in the modern world. Scholars such as Rodney Stark argue that we are currently in the midst of the single greatest religious surge the world has ever seen.[48]

Postsecular scholars widely recognize that secular frames of reference are increasingly incapable of offering an adequate description of social reality as experienced by vast populations in

---

[48] Stark, *Triumph*, 9.

the world, both within and outside of the West.[49] Now that secularism appears to have reached its conceptual and organizational limits, scholars are employing this term 'postsecular' as a way of describing the current and indeed emerging social and cultural conditions in which more and more nations are situated.

We should note that postsecular scholars are generally not talking merely about spiritual renewal or religious revival, which are often notoriously limited and fleeting. Instead, postsecular scholars are aptly aware of what are called *desecularizing* or *counter-secularizing* dynamics in societies, which, as the terms suggest, involve various counterreactions towards secularizing processes and institutions.[50] Postsecular dynamics often involve a reconfiguration of political, cultural, and educational norms around religious beliefs and practices as a response to the secularizing processes of globalization. In other words, postsecularism tends to be socially and culturally holistic; it's not a little religion sprinkled here or there. Though certainly diverse, postsecularity often involves a reorganization of larger social and institutional arrangements, and, therefore, requires a new way of defining and describing societies exemplative of such desecularizing or counter-secularizing dynamics.

With that said, few nations are exemplifying postsecular trends today than the Republic of Georgia, at the heart of which is the revived Georgian Orthodox Church. What happened is that after the dissolution of the Soviet Union on Christmas of 1991, the Georgian Orthodox Church emerged as the single most trusted, respected, and influential institution in Georgian society. As

---

[49] See, for example, Joseph A. Camilleri, "Postsecular discourse in an 'age of transition'," *Review of International Studies* 38 (2012): 1019-1039.
[50] Vyacheslav Karpov, "Desecularization: A Conceptual Framework," *Journal of Church and State* Vol. 52, Issue 2, (March 2010): 232-270.

such, the Georgian Orthodox Church has since filled the mass vacuum that was left with the collapse of communism.

The population of Georgia has consistently been ranked as one of the most religious in the world. Eighty-five percent of the population claims to be Orthodox Christian, with an average weekly church attendance rate of 20 percent, a historic high among European nations.[51] Just to give you an idea of the national commitment to the Georgian Orthodox Church, a recent poll found that 75 percent of respondents said that they would never vote for a political party that was critical of the Georgian Orthodox Church.[52] Needless to say, Georgian politicians are constantly posturing to be seen as pro-Christianity and pro-Orthodox Church; in fact, a politician would have little political legitimacy if they were not in some way endorsed by the Church. In short, after decades of communist rule, the Georgian Orthodox Church has become the symbol of national revival for Georgians.

This cooperation between the church and state has been going on now for some time. Georgia has been a Christian nation since the fourth century when it was the Georgian Kingdom of Kartli. But with the advent of the modern period and ideologically-soaked twentieth century, their Christian status was overshadowed for decades under the imprisoning storm clouds of atheistic communism. Once those clouds were lifted, the Church almost instantly became recognized as an indispensable, moral, spiritual, and cultural foundation for the rebuilding of the nation. And so, in the mid-1990s, then-president Eduard Shevardnadze made an informal deal recognizing the public significance of the Church and the

---

[51] http://georgiatoday.ge/news/7177/Christianity-in-Georgia%3A-The-Resilience-of-a-Faith-%26-Nation.
[52] https://www.opendemocracy.net/od-russia/eka-chitanava/georgia-s-politics-of-piety.

benefits bestowed upon it; and since then, the church's influence has only grown in the political arena.

For example, one of the most significant developments that have taken place of late is what's been considered more or less the Christianization of Georgia's public school system, after decades of Soviet-inspired atheism. The public school system of Georgia now features Orthodox Christianity as part of its curriculum, and the students often engage in Orthodox prayers with icons and crucifixes adorning the hallways and classrooms. This Christianization or perhaps better re-Christianization of the public school system was actually threatened back in 2012 by the then pro-Western, pro-EU, pro-secular government which sought to take Eastern Orthodox curriculum out of the public schools.[53] Such measures only provoked a massive backlash, galvanizing the Orthodox Church and activist groups such as the Orthodox Parents' Union to mobilize significant resistance against these secularizing efforts. When the elections of 2012 came along, a far more traditionalist party known as the Georgian Dream was elected overwhelmingly, and they immediately reinstituted Eastern Orthodox education into the public schools. Once again, it was the Orthodox Church that became a bulwark defending symbols of Georgian Christian nationalism against globalizing tendencies that sought to re-secularize the nation.

As we noted above, we've also seen extraordinary success surrounding the Georgian Orthodox Church's campaign to revitalize the family. For a number of years, Georgia has had one of the lowest birthrates in Eastern Europe. And so, Patriarch Ilia II began a campaign where he promised to personally baptize the

---

[53] https://www.bbc.com/news/world-europe-32595514.

third or higher child of married Orthodox couples.[54] This was back in 2008, and since then, to the astonishment of demographers, Georgia has gone from having one of the lowest birthrates in Eastern Europe to now actually one of the highest.[55]

Another area of interest is in how Georgian officials try to negotiate and comply with the requirements and norms of the larger but thoroughly secular European Union while maintaining their postsecular identity. I think this is actually a very interesting field of inquiry for postsecular studies: How does a nation dedicated to postsecular rearrangements deal faithfully with a nation or organization dedicated to maintaining secular norms and requirements? Take, for example, the way Georgia handled the European Union's requirement that all states applying for an EU-recognized visa liberalization, which requires member states to have laws that prevent discrimination on the basis of sexual orientation and gender identity. And so, Georgia's parliament put together a bill under the close watch of the Georgian Orthodox Church that provided a law compatible with the EU's requirements, but devoid of any stated penalties for those who violated the law. Simply put, while it was now illegal to discriminate against homosexuals and transgenders, there was no express punishment for those who would be found guilty of such discrimination. Moreover, there was a further provision that affirms that no law can be construed to contradict the constitutional agreement of cooperation between the state and the Orthodox Church of Georgia. So, here we have an interesting example of postsecular international relations, where agreement

[54] https://journeytoorthodoxy.com/2019/01/patriarch-ilia-of-georgia-baptizes-630-children-in-57th-mass-baptism-ceremony/.
[55] https://www.theguardian.com/world/2012/may/06/georgian-orthodox-church-mass-baptisms.

and compliance with transnational secular requirements remain consistent with a nation's postsecular cultural identity.

What are some takeaways from all of this? Well, I think Georgia and many other nations in Central and Eastern Europe are showing us what desecularization looks like at multiple levels of society and culture. In other words, we moderns all too often think of religion or the Christian faith in purely personal and subjective terms. Such personalized sensibilities exemplify the ways in which religion evolved after the establishment of the Westphalian Order in the seventeenth century. Through the secularizing influence of the Enlightenment, it became commonplace to think of religion as something that affected people solely at what we might call a micro-level, that is, the level of the individual human person, with little relevance beyond the personal and subjective. But what postsecular scholars are noticing is that more and more societies like Georgia are evidencing desecularizing processes at higher levels, such as the meso-level of institutions and the macro-level of society itself. Indeed, some scholars are even recognizing a burgeoning postsecularism at what's called the mega-level, at the level of international relations and transnational interrelationships, as we saw with the ways in which Georgia deals with the demands of Brussels. Because desecularizing or counter-secularizing processes respond to the pervasiveness of secular norms and dynamics, these processes inevitably reconfigure virtually every aspect of demographic, economic, political, and cultural life within a nation, and increasingly, even relations between nations, promising what many are calling a postsecular international or world order.[56] The emergence of a postsecular age indicates that religion can no

---

[56] L. Mavelli (ed.), Towards a Postsecular International Politics: New Forms of Community, Identity, and Power (New York: Palgrave Macmillan), 2014.

longer be thought of in subjective privatized terms; religion is in point of fact once again reorganizing the totality of social and cultural life in ways that will have profound effects for the foreseeable future.

As we saw above, there are a number of ways in which the Georgian Orthodox Church is fulfilling just such a role, playing a major political force in the renewal of the Republic of Georgia after decades of Soviet-inspired communism. At the heart of Georgia, we're seeing a major religious revival that has effectively desecularized much of Georgian society and awakened a renewed nationalism, and as such, stands strong against the secularizing tendencies and anti-cultural processes of transnational Brussels-based globalization. As the world becomes more and more postglobalist and postsecular, Georgia is a shining example of the kind of nation that we will see many more of in the years ahead.

CHAPTER 7

Raising a Godly Generation:
The Hungarian Vision for
Christian Schools

I have been an educator now for over 20 years. During that time, some 17 years ago, I was introduced to the renaissance of classical Christian education. I immediately fell in love; as a pedagogy that encultures students in the True, the Good, and the Beautiful through the acquisition of wisdom and virtue, classical education has no equal. The educators of old were keenly aware that education is not merely *informative,* as if the teacher were simply the transmitter of information; rather, education is profoundly and deeply *formative.* Education shapes and molds students into a human ideal particular to the culture in which they are taught. For the Greeks and Romans, Christians and Jews, education was always *enculturation.*

The term 'education' comes from the Latin *ēducō* which means both "I educate, I train" and "I lead forth." The obvious question with regard to the meaning of education is rather evident: if education means 'to lead forth,' then to what and to where are our children being led? The rather simple answer to this question is that children are always being led to embrace and become a part of a wider culture of which education is an intrinsic part. Students don't just learn math and science and disinterested facts in school; they learn language, customs, and calendars; they acquire dispositions, inclinations, and habits, all of which reflect and indeed initiate the student into the norms and expectations of a wider culture. Education is always enculturation.

And so, as we examine the trends indicating a coming Christian majority, the conservative-based reform of education is an extremely important part of the sustainability of such trends since education is all about enculturating students into a particular vision of what it means to be human. While there are very encouraging signs of educational renewal going on, particularly in the United States with the renaissance of classical education, few nations are taking this conservative vision of education as seriously as the educational reforms currently underway in the nation of Hungary.

Shortly after his massive landslide win in April of 2018, a victory that gave him his third-straight term as prime minister, Viktor Orban announced his vision to build Hungary into what he called a 'Christian democracy.' Among the distinctives of a Christian democracy, Orban has focused on a renewed cooperation between church and state in the preservation of their national customs, cultures, and traditions; the protection of the nations' borders so as to protect Hungary's unique values; a diverse application of economic nationalism as an extension of national identity; and a renewed committed to fostering and furthering the natural family for a flourishing future.[57] But amidst these grand social goals, it's

---

[57] For a development of Orban's vision of a Christian democracy, see my *The New Nationalism: How the Populist Right is Defeating Globalism and Awakening a New Political Order* (Newark, DE: Turley Talks Publishing), 2018.

the reforms in Hungary's K-12 education system that just may have the most significant impact for the coming Christian majority.

János Lázár, a very influential Hungarian politician and member of Viktor Orban's cabinet, recently remarked that the single most important institutions of education in Hungary are the Christian parochial schools, and he went on to say that the primary goal of education in Hungary is officially now to raise good Christians and good Hungarians. In fact, he made the argument that "the lesson of the last 1,000 years is that the nation can endure only through religious educational institutions."[58]

Now, as part of that vision, Hungary is transferring many of its public schools over to the Christian church.[59] As a result, the number of Christian parochial schools has been growing quite rapidly, especially since Viktor Orban successfully nationalized the schools that were formerly run by local municipalities. Just to give you an idea of the surge in Christian education in Hungary: In 2010, there were a total of 572 church-operated schools; today, that number has more than doubled to over 1,300! Note that the number of church operated schools has doubled in just a matter of eight years. In 2010, there were just over 112,000 students attending parochial schools; today their number has reached nearly 210,000. There are even some communities in Hungary that *only* have Christian schools; in other words, the parochial school is their only school of choice. This trend of only church-run schools, particularly in small towns and villages, has been going on for some time now. Between 2001 and 2011, those attending church-run schools in towns and villages increased 60 percent, and after Viktor Orban and his Fidesz Party's win in

---

[58] http://hungarianspectrum.org/2017/09/01/the-orban-governments-penchant-for-religious-educational-institutions/.

[59] http://www.tfp.org/hungary-hands-over-public-schools-to-religious-institutions-2/.

2010, that number increased again from 2011 and 2014 by an additional 47 percent.[60] According to a recent study, there are nearly 100 villages and 30 larger towns without a single secular public school.[61] The secular public school is fast becoming the minority form of education in Hungary.

Now, by all accounts, these Christian schools are far and away better than secular public schools. Beyond just the moral teachings and the strong sense of sacred nationalism that's taught in most parochial schools, they also receive far more money than do public schools, often times twice the money. In recent years, parochial schools get three times the funding per student than standard public schools. In addition, because they are run by churches and not directly by the state, they can choose their own textbooks and curriculum and have far more control over which students they will accept, thus, they can institute very strict disciplinary standards as well as academic standards.

In fact, the government in Hungary plans on spending billions on parochial education over the coming years. For example, they are giving significant grants to the Order of Piarists, which is perhaps the oldest Catholic educational order, for their school system. So, there's no question that Hungary is committed to educating students in Orban's vision for a Christian democracy.

Now, the ramifications for this transference from secular schools to parochial schools for future generations in Hungary really can't be exaggerated. The purpose of secular schools up to this point has not been one of conveying mere religious neutrality, which, of course, is the foundational justification for secularized public schooling. Instead, Orban's government largely recognizes that

---

[60] https://budapestbeacon.com/church-schools-taking-over-in-hungarys-poorer-regions/.
[61] http://hungarianspectrum.org/2017/09/01/the-orban-governments-penchant-for-religious-educational-institutions/.

secularized public schooling is actually about enculturating students in the values of globalism and multiculturalism; Hungarian officials are increasingly aware that secularized schooling is not about religious neutrality; it is about the supremacy of the values of globalism and training students to be disposed towards such values. From what we can gather from the developments in education throughout Hungary, that globalist educational vision is dead. A new vision, one that reveres and protects culture, custom, and tradition rooted in the classical and Christian frames of reference of Western civilization, is rising throughout Hungary, as well as in Poland and increasingly throughout Central Europe, which, in turn, is fostering a European renaissance that promises to transform the lives of students and citizenship for generations to come.

CHAPTER 8

Holy Rus': The Rebirth of Orthodox Civilization in the New Russia

In 2017, an important and insightful book was published entitled *Holy Rus': The Rebirth of Orthodoxy in the New Russia*. The author was John Burgess, a professor of systematic theology at Pittsburgh Theological Seminary. Over the last several years, Burgess made a number of trips to Russia, lived in Moscow and St. Petersburg, and participated in pilgrimages to a number of Russian Orthodoxy's most important monasteries, parishes, and holy sites. His book documents for us a personal tour, albeit from a Protestant professor, of the rebirth of Orthodoxy and Orthodox civilization in New Russia. Personal yet erudite, the study exemplifies the author's admiration as well as a caution for this societal renaissance, which appears to be an exemplar of the kind of re-Christianization that's currently underway in a number of formerly Byzantine and Western nations.

Burgess begins with a brief social and cultural landscape of Russian society prior to the 1917 October Revolution, a landscape dominated by the Russian Orthodox Church. Ninety percent of the nation's population participated at least once a year in the Orthodox Church's sacraments. Fifty thousand parishes, 25,000 chapels, 1,000 monasteries, 60 seminaries, and four theological academies covered the land. And sitting enthroned as the great benefactor and protector of the church was the tsar in all of his glory and majesty. There was simply no other Orthodox nation that could even compare with Holy Rus.'

Burgess notes that what happened after the communist revolution was simply unprecedented in Christian history. The church suffered persecution on a scale the likes of which had never been seen in history. By the end of Stalin's reign of terror, the Orthodox Church was virtually eliminated; what was once the most dominant social and cultural force in all of Russia had been reduced to mere rubble, very much like the tsar. Seemingly overnight, the 1,000 monasteries were all closed, and the theological schools met the same fate. Only four bishops remained in office. And the 50,000 parishes were reduced to a mere few hundred. It's estimated that over 85 percent of clergy and monastics had been arrested and were consigned to die in work camps. As many as 300,000 people associated with the church were killed.

Now, in one of the great ironies of history, it was the German invasion of the Soviet Union in 1941 that saved the church from complete annihilation. And one of the ways that Stalin and his generals tried to win popular support for their war on Hitler was to allow some of these churches and monasteries to reopen. By the end of the war, the church had 15,000 parishes, 100 monasteries, and 8 seminaries. The Khrushchev years, unfortunately, involved a renewed effort to enculturate the population in atheism, and the church began to dwindle to half the amount of churches, 16 monasteries, and just a couple of seminaries.

Nevertheless, when the Soviet Union fell, it is astonishing that 30 percent of the population still referred to themselves as Russian

Orthodox. Here's something even more amazing: after nearly 70 years of deliberate and dogmatic atheism taught in Soviet schools and universities, a survey taken shortly after the fall of the Soviet Union found that only 6 percent of the population identified themselves as atheists; that's 1 percent more than the global average [cite Stark]. Seventy years of deliberate and dogmatic atheistic education resulted in a 1 percent difference from the global average of atheists.

According to Burgess, the collapse of the Soviet Union evoked within many Russians a yearning to understand and know what made Russia uniquely "Russia." How was Russia different from Europe and other Western nations? And more and more, it appeared that the Russian Orthodox Church had the answer to this question. The Russian Orthodox Church does not merely symbolize a church identity; it symbolizes a political identity, indeed a full-blown national identity. It sees itself as being given by God the unique role in preserving the distinctively Eastern Orthodox vision of heaven on earth for all the world to see and indeed participate in. And so, the Russian Orthodox Church understands its renewed mission as twofold: it would strive to invite all Russians into a personal faith and moral transformation on the one hand and provide a sense of national distinctiveness and destiny on the other. In short, as Burgess points out, Soviet communism has indeed been replaced with Russian Orthodoxy.

And the results speak for themselves: today, as of 2015, the church has grown to more than 35,000 parishes, 800 monasteries, and innumerable welfare and educational ministries spread throughout the nation. There are recent reports that we are seeing the highest numbers ever recorded now training for the priesthood in the church's 261 dioceses. There are currently nearly 1,600 seminarians newly enrolled in preparation for ordination to the priesthood in Russia, which represents a 20 percent increase from the new enrollments from last year in 2016. And it brings the total seminarians to about 6,000 now preparing for ordination; it's just a stunning number.[62] The most recent surveys corroborate that nearly 70 percent of the Russian population see themselves as either religious or very religious, and an astonishing 93 percent affirm their support and respect for the Russian Orthodox Church and Orthodox Christians. Perhaps most surprisingly, a recent survey found that 30 percent of Russians would like to see a return to some kind of monarchical rule comparable to the Tsars.[63]

Moreover, the Orthodox Church has even made its way into domestic political policy in something called *spiritual security*. Burgess doesn't get into this aspect so much, but I think it's very important. Spiritual security is considered a subset of national security in a number of policy documents issued by President Putin's administration, which is designed as a primary measure by which traditional Russian values embodied particularly by the Russian Orthodox Church can be protected and perpetuated in the midst of globalized assaults.[64] It's fully recognized that globalization involves radically detraditionalizing forces that dis-embed time and space away from localized and customary interpretation and control and re-embeds them in transnational consumer-based interpretations. And so, the Russian policy of spiritual security is taking the secular detraditionalizing forces of globalization very seriously. In 2000, the National Security Concept of Russia stated that the assurance of the Russian

---

[62] https://www.christiantoday.com/article/astonishing-church-growth-in-russia-sees-record-number-training-for-priesthood/110512.htm.
[63] https://www.france24.com/en/20171029-century-after-revolution-russians-crave-return-tsar.
[64] Julie Elkner, "Spiritual Security in Putin's Russia," available at http://historyandpolicy.org/papers/ policy-paper-26.html.

Federation's national security included protecting the nation's cultural, spiritual, and moral legacy and the historical traditions and standards of public life. There has to be a state policy that maintains the population's spiritual and moral welfare. Vladimir Putin has drawn a very tight connection between religion, culture, and nationality; so much so that back in 2002, the Moscow Patriarch Alexey II consecrated an Orthodox Church on the grounds of the Lubianka headquarters of the Federal Security Agency, which was formerly known as the KGB. And the key here was the symbolic gesture of bringing together the church and state in maintaining the distinctively Christian identity of Russia. The Russian Patriarch made it very clear that the ceremony solidified the joint effort between departments of the government and the Russian Orthodox Church to maintain the spiritual security of the Russian population.

Vladimir Putin has instituted this spiritual security in a number of ways. In June of 2013, Putin signed into law Article 148 of the Russian criminal code, which threatens prison sentences of up to three years for "insulting the feelings of Christian believers."[65] Such laws against offending the church were used to incarcerate the punk rock band Pussy Riot when they desecrated two churches with lewd and inappropriate behavior. And on the very day that law was passed, another law was approved that prohibits so-called "homosexual propaganda" in Russia. In addition, Putin has banned abortion ads, and signed legislation banning abortion after 12 weeks of pregnancy, all while the Russian Orthodox Church is calling for an all-out ban of abortions.

The result is that Russia is one of the leading nations in the process of re-Christianization that's currently going on in nations

---

[65] John Anderson, Conservative Christian Politics in Russia and the United States: Dreaming of Christian Nations (London: Routledge, 2015), 82.

such as Poland, Hungary, Georgia, and many others. As Burgess' personal account suggests, the reawakening of Christian civilization in Russia is nothing short of a miracle, blessed by God to bear witness to the dawning or revitalization of Christian civilization as more and more nations turn away from the dying and wilting secular world order of globalization and turn back towards the resurgence of Christian faith, culture, and society. *This* is the coming Christian majority.

Thank you again for purchasing this book!

I hope this book encouraged you by showing you the exciting ways demographics and politics are converging to create a new Christian majority in the West.

If you enjoyed this book, then I'd like to ask you for a favor: Would you be kind enough to leave a review for this book on Amazon? I would so greatly appreciate it!

Thank you so much, and may God richly bless you!

Steve Turley

www.turleytalks.com

Check Out My Other Books

Below you'll find some of my other popular books that are popular on Amazon. Simply go to the links below to check them out. Alternatively, you can visit my author page on Amazon to see my other works.

- *The New Nationalism: How the Populist Right is Defeating Globalism and Awakening a New Political Order* https://amzn.to/2WEP11u

- *The Triumph of Tradition: How the Resurgence of Religion is Reawakening a Conservative World* https://amzn.to/2xieNO3

- *Classical vs. Modern Education: A Vision from C.S. Lewis* http://amzn.to/2opDZju

- *President Trump and Our Post-Secular Future: How the 2016 Election Signals the Dawning of a Conservative Nationalist Age* http://amzn.to/2B87Q22

- *Gazing: Encountering the Mystery of Art* https://amzn.to/2yKi6k9

- *Beauty Matters: Creating a High Aesthetic in School Culture* https://amzn.to/2L8Ejd7

- *Ever After: How to Overcome Cynical Students with the Role of Wonder in Education* http://amzn.to/2jbJI78

- *Movies and the Moral Imagination: Finding Paradise in Films* http://amzn.to/2zjghJj

- *Health Care Sharing Ministries: How Christians are Revolutionizing Medical Cost and Care* http://amzn.to/2B2Q8B2

- *The Face of Infinite of Love: Athanasius on the Incarnation* http://amzn.to/2oxULNM

- *Stressed Out: Learn How an Ancient Christian Practice Can Relieve Stress and Overcome Anxiety* http://amzn.to/2kFzcpc

- *Wise Choice: Six Steps to Godly Decision Making* http://amzn.to/2qy3C2Z

- *Awakening Wonder: A Classical Guide to Truth, Goodness, and Beauty* http://amzn.to/2ziKR5H

- *Worldview Guide for* A Christmas Carol http://amzn.to/2BCcKHO

- *The Ritualized Revelation of the Messianic Age: Washings and Meals in Galatians and 1 Corinthians* http://amzn.to/2B0mGvf

If the links do not work, for whatever reason, you can simply search for these titles on the Amazon website to find them.

About www.TurleyTalks.com

Are we seeing the revitalization of Christian civilization?

For decades, the world has been dominated by a process known as globalization, an economic and political system that hollows out and erodes a culture's traditions, customs, and religions, all the while conditioning populations to rely on the expertise of a tiny class of technocrats for every aspect of their social and economic lives.

Until now.

All over the world, there's been a massive blowback against the anti-cultural processes of globalization and its secular aristocracy. From Russia to Europe and now in the U.S., citizens are rising up and reasserting their religion, culture, and nation as mechanisms of resistance against the dehumanizing tendencies of secularism and globalism.

And it's just the beginning.

The secular world is at its brink, and a new traditionalist age is rising.

Join me each week as we examine these worldwide trends, discover answers to today's toughest challenges, and together learn to live in the present in light of even better things to come.

So hop on over to www.TurleyTalks.com and have a look around. Make sure to sign-up for our weekly Email Newsletter where you'll get lots of free giveaways, private Q&As, and tons of great content. Check out our YouTube channel (www.youtube.com/c/DrSteveTurley) where you'll understand current events in light of conservative trends to help you flourish in your personal and professional life. And of course, 'Like' us on Facebook and follow us on Twitter.

Thank you so much for your support and for your part in this cultural renewal.

About the Author

Steve Turley (PhD, Durham University) is an internationally recognized scholar, speaker, and classical guitarist. He is the author of over a dozen books, including *Classical vs. Modern Education: A Vision from C.S. Lewis, Awakening Wonder: A Classical Guide to Truth, Goodness, and Beauty*, and *The Ritualized Revelation of the Messianic Age: Washings and Meals in Galatians and 1 Corinthians*. Steve's popular YouTube channel showcases weekly his expertise in the rise of nationalism, populism, and traditionalism throughout the world, and his podcasts and writings on civilization, society, culture, education, and the arts are widely accessed at TurleyTalks.com. He is a faculty member at Tall Oaks Classical School in Bear, DE, where he teaches Theology and Rhetoric, and was formerly Professor of Fine Arts at Eastern University. Steve lectures at universities, conferences, and churches throughout the U.S. and abroad. His research and writings have appeared in such journals as *Christianity and Literature, Calvin Theological Journal, First Things, Touchstone*, and *The Chesterton Review*. He and his wife, Akiko, have four children and live in Newark, DE, where they together enjoy fishing, gardening, and watching *Duck Dynasty* marathons.

Made in the USA
Monee, IL
08 August 2020